T0358091

1

Some people love the ocean. Some people love the mountains. I love the desert.

Knowledge Books and Software

3

When I was a kid, I lived on a cattle station near the desert. It was in the country of the Anmatjere people.

Knowledge Books and Software

When I left school, I became a 'sparkie'. This is an electrician. My brother and I got a job fixing an old roadhouse in the desert.

6

7

The old roadhouse had burned down a few years ago. It was just a big pile of old tin and bricks. There was hardly anything left.

Knowledge Books and Software

The place was like a junk yard. It was very old and falling down. There was no roof on the toilet. You could sit and see the stars at night. It was on a rough, dusty road with some rusty, old cars. Our car nearly fell to bits on the way there!

Knowledge Books and Software

11

We fixed the electrical generator. This gave us power. We also ran a new water pipe from far away so people could live there again.

Knowledge Books and Software

13

Knowledge Books and Software

We started fixing up the old roadhouse. It was going to be a big job. We were on our own but we had visits from a dingo.

15

We built a new shop and petrol pumps. We could now start to sell food and petrol. We got the petrol by the road train.

16

17

There were many First Nations people living on their country. I got to know many of these people. We became good friends.

Knowledge Books and Software

19

I helped the families nearby to get a good water supply. Water was very important and hard to get out there. It was needed for drinking, washing and cooking.

Knowledge Books and Software

One day, the elder came to talk to me. I felt his true kindness like it was my own Dad. He said I was ready for my new name. The elder showed me all the sacred sites where his ancestors used to visit. I was now called Jungala.

Knowledge Books and Software

Word bank

ocean

mountains

desert

station

Anmatjere

country

people

electrician

roadhouse

electrical

generator

dingo

petrol

friends

important

elder

sacred

ancestors

Jungala

Knowledge Books and Software